LUXEMBOURG CITY

TRAVEL GUIDE

2023

The Ultimate Guide to exploring the capital city of Luxembourg: Discover the culture and explore the great sights and hidden gems of Luxembourg City

Christopher Levell

Copyright

Christopher Levell © 2023. All rights reserved

Before this document is duplicated or reproduced in any manner, the publisher's consent must be gained.

Therefore, the contents within can neither be stored electronically, transferred, nor kept in a database. Neither in part nor in full can the document be copied, scanned, faxed, or retained without approval from the publisher or creator.

TABLE OF CONTENTS

1. INTRODUCTION
About This Guide
Overview of Luxembourg City
History of Luxembourg City
Geography and Climate
Getting to Luxembourg City
Travel Tips and Useful Information
2. EXPLORING LUXEMBOURG CITY
Top Attractions
Districts and Neighborhoods
Gardens and Parks
Luxembourg City's shopping
Eating and entertainment
3. ACTIVITIES AND DAY TRIPS
4. PRACTICAL INFORMATION
Options for Accommodation
Luxembourg City's transport
Currency Exchange and Money
Emergency and Safety Contacts
Communication and Language
Etiquette & Customs
5. CULTURAL EXPERIENCES
6. TIPS FOR SUSTAINABLE VISIT
7. USEFUL PHRASES AND VOCABULARIES
7. CONCLUSION
8. APPENDIX

Luxembourg city

Luxembourg city

4

1. INTRODUCTION

About This Guide

Welcome to the thorough Luxembourg City tourist guide! This book is intended to provide you with all the necessary information you need to make the most of your visit to this stunning capital city, whether you are a first-time tourist or an experienced traveler. Every style of traveler may find something to enjoy in Luxembourg City, from historical sites to cultural experiences, scenic beauty, and gastronomic pleasures. So let's dig into this tour and learn more about Luxembourg City's beauties!

Overview of Luxembourg City

The Grand Duchy of Luxembourg's capital, Luxembourg metropolis, is a bustling, multicultural metropolis tucked away in the center of Europe. Visitors from over the globe are enthralled by it because of its extensive history, stunning architecture, and contemporary appeal. The Ville Haute (Upper Town), the city's UNESCO-listed historic core, is recognised for being positioned atop a magnificent cliff and providing spectacular panoramic views. A cultural city that values variety and innovation, Luxembourg City is also the nation's political and economic center.

History of Luxembourg City

The history of Luxembourg City, which spans more than a thousand years, is intriguing. Since its founding in 963, it has seen the rise and fall of several empires, been a major player in European politics, and acted as a strategic bastion for many years. The city's history is evident wherever you look, from medieval defenses to the remnants of the renowned Casemates du Bock. After World War II, various international organizations made Luxembourg City its headquarters, earning the city recognition as a symbol of peace.

Geography and Climate

Luxembourg City provides a distinctive fusion of rural beauty and urban growth. It is located in a lovely valley surrounded by undulating hills. The city, which straddles the Alzette River, is distinguished by its mountainous topography, lovely cobblestone lanes, and verdant greenery. With warm summers and cold winters, Luxembourg City has a temperate climate. The best times to stroll about the city and take in its outdoor sights are in the warm spring and fall seasons.

Getting to Luxembourg City

The city of Luxembourg is well-connected and simple to get there via a variety of means of transportation. The primary entry point for foreign travelers is the Luxembourg Findel Airport, which is just 6 kilometers from the city center. It acts as a hub for connecting flights and provides direct flights to significant European destinations. Additionally, there are regular rail connections from Luxembourg City to nearby nations including Belgium, France, and Germany. Major European cities are easily accessible by high-speed trains. It is simple to get about the city because of the effective public transport infrastructure in the area, which includes buses and trams.

Travel Tips and Useful Information

- **Currency**: The Euro (EUR) is the official unit of exchange in Luxembourg City.
- **Language**: Although Luxembourgish is the official language, the majority of the population also speaks French and German. Most people can communicate in English, particularly in touristy locations.
- **Safety**: With low crime rates, Luxembourg City is regarded as a safe place to visit. However, it's always a good idea to use common sense safety measures and pay attention to your surroundings.
- **Local customs:** Luxembourgers are renowned for being kind and

courteous. It is polite to shake hands when you meet someone and act respectfully.

- **Tipping**: Tipping is not required in Luxembourg since a service fee is often tacked on to the bill. To compensate for great service, it's customary to round up the total or offer a little tip.
- **Electricity:** If you're traveling from a different location, you may require an adaptor since the typical voltage is 230V and the plugs are of the European kind.

You're prepared to start your trip to Luxembourg City after considering these travel advice and helpful facts. Prepare to be enthralled by the charming city's rich history, gorgeous architecture, and welcoming people. Have a good time!

2. EXPLORING LUXEMBOURG CITY

Luxembourg City is a veritable gold mine of landmarks, communities, green spaces, and exciting cultural opportunities. Every tourist will find something to fascinate them, from attractive neighborhoods to historical sites. Let's explore the finest sights, areas, parks, shops, restaurants, and nightlife that make Luxembourg City a genuinely memorable vacation destination.

Top Attractions

1. Place d'Armes, France

Place d'Armes is a lively area surrounded by cafes, restaurants, and stores in the center of Luxembourg City. This popular meeting spot is ideal for people-watching and taking in the energetic energy of the city. To further enhance its appeal, the area often holds events and outdoor performances.

2. Grand Ducal Palace

For those who like history and architecture, a trip to the Grand Ducal Palace is a need. The Grand Duke of Luxembourg's formal home is this opulent building. Although the palace is closed to the public throughout the year, guided tours are offered in the summer, giving guests the chance to explore the lavish interiors and discover more about the country's royalty.

3. Notre-Dame Cathedral

The beautiful Gothic Notre Dame Cathedral dominates Luxembourg City's skyline. It is a notable religious and cultural monument due to its beautiful architecture, exquisite stained glass windows, and serene atmosphere. You'll discover exquisitely built chapels and John the Blind, the King of Bohemia,'s tomb within.

4. Du Bock Casemates

Explore the Casemates du Bock, a vast system of subterranean tunnels and fortresses, and get ready to go back in time. These tunnels, which were constructed in the 17th century as a defensive stronghold, provide an intriguing look into Luxembourg

City's military past. Panorama views of the city are offered by the casemates, and fascinating histories are revealed during guided tours.

5. Adolphe Bridge

The Adolphe Bridge, which spans the Pétrusse Valley, is a well-known image of Luxembourg City. Builtin the early 20th century, this magnificent arched bridge provides wonderful views of the city skyline and the lovely Pétrusse Valley below. Cross the bridge casually and take in the expansive views of the city while taking unforgettable photos.

6. MUDAM (Museum of Modern Art)

The Kirchberg neighborhood's Museum of Modern Art (MUDAM) is sure to captivate art lovers. This museum of modern art features a varied collection of modern artwork from across the world and Luxembourg, including photographs, paintings, sculptures, installations, and multimedia displays. The museum is a must-visit for art enthusiasts due to its stunning architecture and often changing exhibits.

7. National Museum of Art and History

Visit the National Museum of History and Art to immerse yourself in Luxembourg's lengthy past. This comprehensive museum has a sizable collection that ranges from the ancient to the present periods. Learn about the nation's history, culture, and creative accomplishments by exploring archaeological artifacts, historical records, great art, and interactive exhibits.

Districts and Neighborhoods

1. Upper Town/Ville Haute

The Ville Haute, or Upper Town, is the historic core of Luxembourg City and is perched on a magnificent cliff. With its cobblestone lanes, quaint squares, and intact medieval buildings, this UNESCO-listed neighborhood is a treat to explore. Explore ancient locations including

Saint Michael's Church, Place Guillaume II, and the Corniche, a charming promenade with sweeping views of the Alzette Valley.

2. Grund

The Grund neighborhood, which is tucked away at the base of the city's cliffs, is charming and scenic. Explore its confined alleyways and take in historic homes, some of which have been wonderfully renovated. Grund is home to the charming Alzette River, where you may go for a relaxing stroll along its banks. The monastery of Neumünster, a cultural hub located in a historic Benedictine monastery, is a must-see.

3. Kirchberg

Kirchberg, the contemporary commercial sector of Luxembourg City, is where several institutions of the European Union are located. The European Investment Bank and the European Court of Justice, both of which have futuristic architecture, are located in this upscale, international neighborhood. Visit the Philharmonie Luxembourg, a marvel of architecture known for its top-notch shows and concerts.

4. Clausen

A bustling neighborhood immediately outside the city center is called Clausen. Clausen, a city well-known for its vibrant nightlife, is teeming with taverns, pubs, and clubs. With its small alleys and old houses, this district has kept its identity as a working-class neighborhood. Enjoy a night out and take in the lively social scene of the city.

Gardens and Parks

Numerous parks and gardens in Luxembourg City provide a pleasant respite from the city's bustle. Here are some noteworthy parks worth visiting:

- **Pétrusse Valley Park:** Pétrusse Valley Park is a beautiful park with lovely walking routes, elegant bridges, and peaceful picnic areas. It is situated under the city's defenses.

- **Luxembourg City Park**: This well-kept park, located close to the city center, has lovely flower displays, fountains, and tranquil walks.

- **Edmund Klein Park**: Edmund Klein Park is a paradise for nature lovers and offers beautiful views of the city. It is well-known for its lovely rose garden.

Luxembourg City's shopping

Luxurious brands, chic local markets, and contemporary shops combine to make shopping in Luxembourg City a joy. Avenue de la Liberté and Rue Philippe II, which are pedestrianized, are the primary shopping districts; here, you'll discover a variety of international fashion labels, designer boutiques, upscale jewelry shops and speciality stores selling regional handcrafted goods. Don't forget to browse the lively outdoor markets, such as the weekly farmers' market at Place Guillaume II, where you can enjoy regional specialities and locally grown products.

Eating and entertainment

The varied selection of eating choices in Luxembourg City reflects the city's cosmopolitan culture and caters to a wide range of preferences. You'll discover a variety of eateries, cafés, and bistros serving everything from local specialities to global flavors. Discover quaint restaurants providing filling regional delicacies like Gromperekichelcher (potato fritters) and Judd mat Gaardebounen (smoked pork with broad beans) while exploring the Old Town's picturesque alleyways. The fashionable restaurants, pubs, and clubs in Kirchberg and Clausen are well-known for their vibrant nightlife, where you can relax and take in live music or DJ performances.

The city of Luxembourg is a place where the past, present, and future coexist together. Every visitor to Luxembourg City is guaranteed an engaging and remarkable experience thanks to the city's compelling attractions, different neighborhoods, attractive parks, and exciting eating and nightlife options.

3. ACTIVITIES AND DAY TRIPS

Numerous excursions and activities are available in Luxembourg City, allowing guests to fully experience the area's rich culture, history, and scenic beauty. There are many ways to maximize your time in and around Luxembourg City, from bike and walking tours to wine-tasting excursions and thrilling day trips. Let's look at some of the best day excursions and activities you should include in your schedule.

1. Tours by bike and on foot

Walking or riding a bike are two of the greatest ways to discover Luxembourg City. The city is walkable and small, making it simple to get about and find its hidden beauties. Learn about the city's history, architecture, and urban legends by taking a guided walking tour. Explore the Old Town's quaint alleyways, take in the fortifications, and stop by famous sites like the Grand Ducal Palace and Notre Dame Cathedral. Rent a bike to explore the city's well-maintained bike trails and picturesque riverfront roads if you prefer to pedal.

2. Nighttime in Luxembourg City

After nightfall, Luxembourg City has a completely different atmosphere, and nighttime exploration is a beautiful experience. Take a nighttime walking tour to see the city lit up and the mesmerizing mood it creates. Explore the elegantly lighted historical structures, savor the peace of Pétrusse Valley Park at night, and take in the stunning views from the city's vantage points. A nighttime boat along the Alzette River is another option for seeing the city's lit bridges and cityscape.

3. Tours of the Moselle Valley's Wineries

The Moselle Valley, which is close to Luxembourg City, is well known for its beautiful vineyards and top-notch wines. Explore the lovely wine towns along the Moselle River by going on a wine-tasting trip. Meet local winemakers, tour vineyards, and taste a selection of wines, including the renowned Rieslings. Take in the beautiful scenery, see how wine is made, and taste the local flavors.

4. Day Trips from Luxembourg City

The central position of Luxembourg City gives it a great starting point for day visits to adjacent destinations. Here are a few well-liked day excursion ideas:

- **Castle Vianden**

Vianden Castle is a magnificent medieval stronghold that takes tourists back in time. It is situated in the charming village of Vianden, not far from Luxembourg City. Discover the castle's well-preserved interior spaces, climb the towers for expansive views, and discover its interesting past. With its quaint cafés, historic homes, and attractive streets, the village of Vianden is worth seeing in and of itself.

- **Achten, Switzerland**

Known as Little Switzerland, the Mullerthal Region includes the lovely village of Echternach. Echternach, known for its medieval abbey and breathtaking natural scenery, provides the ideal fusion of historical significance and outdoor fun. Wander around the ancient town, take a stroll along the banks of the Sûre River, and explore the abbey. With its unusual rock formations, extensive woods, and attractive routes, the Mullerthal Region nearby is a hiker's delight.

- **Region of Mullerthal (Little Switzerland)**

For those who like the outdoors and the natural world, the Mullerthal Region is a real treasure. This charming area in eastern Luxembourg has impressive rock formations, flowing rivers, and lush woods. Explore hiking paths like the Schiessentümpel Trail or the Mullerthal Trail to find undiscovered waterfalls, tight gorges, and breathtaking vistas. Don't overlook famous sites like the Holy Cave and the Schiessentümpel waterfall.

- **The Ardennes**

Visit the Ardennes area, which is renowned for its lush woods, rolling hills, and charming towns, for a more challenging and adventurous day excursion. Discover the historical monuments in the area, such as the Battle of the Bulge memorial sites, by exploring the natural reserves, hiking along beautiful paths, and exploring. Outdoor pursuits like cycling, canoeing, and even spelunking in its limestone caverns are possible in the Ardennes.

Luxembourg City and its surrounds offer a wide range of experiences, whether you like to explore the city on foot, go to the wine region, or take thrilling day excursions. You'll have plenty of chances throughout your vacation to this delightful location to make amazing experiences, from cultural immersions to outdoor excursions.

4. PRACTICAL INFORMATION

It's crucial to have some useful information while organizing your trip to Luxembourg City to guarantee a smooth and pleasurable stay. Being prepared will improve your whole experience in terms of everything from lodging possibilities to transportation, money and currency conversion, safety, language, and customs. Let's go into the specific practical information you should be aware of before your journey.

Options for Accommodation

Every budget and inclination may be accommodated in Luxembourg City's extensive selection of lodging alternatives. Consider some of the following categories:

- **Expensive Hotels**

Luxurious lodgings in Luxembourg City provide first-rate facilities, tasteful accommodations, and first-rate service. They often have dining establishments, spas, exercise facilities, and concierge services on-site. Le Royal, Sofitel Luxembourg Le Grand Ducal, and Hotel Le Place d'Armes are a few of the well-known luxury hotels in the area.

- **Midscale lodging**

Mid-range hotels provide luxurious rooms at a lower cost. These hotels often provide comfortable accommodations, prime locations, and a variety of extras like free Wi-Fi, breakfast, and fitness centers. Novotel Luxembourg Centre, Hotel Parc Belle-Vue, and Hotel Carlton Luxembourg are a few well-liked mid-range choices in Luxembourg City.

- **Affordable lodging**

Travelers on a tight budget may find plenty of economical lodging alternatives in Luxembourg City. These include guesthouses, hostels, and inexpensive hotels. They may have fewer facilities, but they nonetheless provide a convenient and affordable starting point for city exploration. Youth Hostel Luxembourg City, ibis Budget Luxembourg Aéroport, and Hotel Zurich are a few examples of inexpensive lodgings.

Luxembourg City's transport

- **Public Transport**

A sophisticated and effective public transit system serves Luxembourg City. It is simple to get about thanks to the bus network, which serves the whole city and its environs. The timetables are dependable, and the buses are contemporary and pleasant. You may buy tickets from the bus driver or vending machines at bus stops. A Luxembourg Card, which grants unrestricted use of public transit and free admission to several sites, is something to think about.

- **Ridesharing and Cabs**

In Luxembourg City, taxis are widely accessible, and you may locate taxi stands in busy areas. Taxis use a metered system, and there may be extra fees for carrying bags or late-night trips. In Luxembourg City, rideshare services like Uber are also accessible, offering a different and practical mode of transportation.

Currency Exchange and Money

The Euro (EUR) is the official currency of Luxembourg. Banks, exchange offices, and a few hotels provide currency exchange services. You may use your debit or credit card to withdraw cash in Euros from any of the city's many ATMs. Although most hotels, restaurants, and stores take major credit cards, it's always a good idea to have extra cash on hand for smaller businesses or street sellers.

Emergency and Safety Contacts

Travelers are typically thought to feel secure in Luxembourg City. To safeguard your safety, it's always advisable to follow the usual safety procedures. Particularly in congested locations or at popular tourist destinations, keep a watch on your valuables and pay attention to your surroundings. For police, fire, or medical help in an emergency, use the 112 emergency number throughout Europe.

Communication and Language

Luxembourg's three official languages are Luxembourgish, French, and German. In tourist regions, hotels, and restaurants in particular, English is often spoken as well. During your vacation to Luxembourg City, talking in English shouldn't be a problem.

Etiquette & Customs

It is beneficial to be informed of regional traditions and manners while visiting Luxembourg City. Here are some pointers:

- **Salutation**: A simple "bonjour" or "Guten Tag" is fine, and a handshake is common.

- **Punctuality:** Being on time for meetings or social occasions is vital in Luxembourg since punctuality is highly prized there.

- **Tipping**: Tipping is not required in Luxembourg since a service fee is often tacked on to the bill. But it's always nice to give a little more for really great service.

- **Smoking**: Smoking is strictly prohibited in public places in Luxembourg. Generally speaking, smoking is not permitted inside pubs, restaurants, or other public spaces.

- **Dress Code**: The dress code in Luxembourg City is somewhat informal. When visiting formal places or going to cultural events, it is advised to dress well.

You can maximize your time in Luxembourg City by being acquainted with this useful information. Being well-prepared will guarantee a wonderful and trouble-free journey, from selecting the ideal lodging to using the transit system and respecting local traditions.

5. CULTURAL EXPERIENCES

Luxembourg City has a thriving cultural scene in addition to being rich in natural beauty and historical treasures. There are several cultural opportunities to enrich your vacation, including immersing yourself in Luxembourgish culture and tradition, attending festivals and events, seeing museums and galleries, taking in music and theater performances, and savoring regional cuisine. Let's explore Luxembourg City's rich cultural offers.

1. Luxembourgish Traditions and Culture

For a greater knowledge of Luxembourg's identity, immerse yourself in its tradition and culture. Start your exploration of the city's past at Ville Haute (Upper Town), which is home to the Grand Ducal Palace, Notre Dame Cathedral, and Place d'Armes, among other architectural marvels. Discover historical artifacts, works of art, and exhibits that highlight Luxembourg's history and cultural heritage when you visit the National Museum of History and Art.

Spend some time strolling among the nearby neighborhoods, chatting with the welcoming residents, and taking in Luxembourg City's daily life. To experience the local culture, stroll through the crowded streets, visit the markets, and sample some classic Luxembourgish cuisine.

2. Holidays and Other Events

The year-round festivals and events that Luxembourg City offers highlight the city's thriving cultural landscape. One of the highlights is the Summer in the City festival, which presents a variety of outdoor concerts, street performances, and cultural events right in the middle of the city. One of the biggest funfairs in Europe, the Schueberfouer, takes place in the late summer and offers exhilarating rides, interactive games, and authentic food vendors.

With its Christmas markets, Luxembourg City becomes a wintry paradise over the holiday season. Discover the numerous markets dotted about the city, where you can browse for one-of-a-kind presents, indulge in seasonal sweets, and take in the festive ambience.

3. Galleries and Museums

Many museums and galleries in Luxembourg City serve a range of interests. The Museum of Modern Art (MUDAM) offers transient exhibitions by well-known artists and exhibits modern art from all around the globe. The interactive exhibits and multimedia presentations of the Luxembourg City History Museum provide visitors with a glimpse into the city's history.

The Casino Luxembourg - Forum d'Art Contemporain is a contemporary art venue where cutting-edge pieces by national and international artists are on display. The National Museum of Military History offers a thorough examination of Luxembourg's military past for history buffs.

4. Theatre and Music

Luxembourg City has a thriving music and theater culture that presents a variety of shows all year long. For fans of classical music, the Philharmonie Luxembourg is a must-visit venue since it often hosts world-class orchestras, soloists, and chamber music groups. The venue's cutting-edge design and superb acoustics offer an engrossing musical experience.

The Grand Théâtre de Luxembourg offers a varied schedule of theater, opera, and dance shows that mix both national and local artists. For every fan of the performing arts, there is something available, from classical ballet to avant-garde theater.

5. Regional Dishes and Specialty Foods

Any cultural excursion must include sampling the local food. Luxembourgish food mixes Belgian, German, and French elements to create a distinctive gastronomic character. Enjoy classic meals like Quetschentaart (plum tart), Judd mat Gaardebounen (smoked pork with broad beans), and Bouneschlupp (green bean soup).

Visit the local markets, such as the weekly farmers' market at Place Guillaume II, to enjoy fresh local vegetables, artisanal cheeses, and regional delicacies for a genuinely unique experience. Don't forget to drink some Luxembourgish wine with your meals, especially from the Moselle area, which is noted for its Rieslings and Crémants.

Consider taking a cooking lesson or going on a food tour that exposes you to regional specialities and the history behind them if you want to learn more about Luxembourg's culinary heritage.

You'll get a greater understanding of Luxembourg City's history, culture, music, and culinary traditions if you immerse yourself in its artistic, musical, and gastronomic experiences. There are many cultural treasures to explore in this interesting city, from seeing museums and galleries to going to festivals and enjoying local food.

6. TIPS FOR SUSTAINABLE VISIT

We as travelers must think about how our trips affect the environment and work towards sustainable practices. With its dedication to environmental preservation and sustainability, Luxembourg City offers several alternatives for visitors to travel more sustainably and responsibly. Here are some suggestions for more environmentally friendly travel to Luxembourg City.

1. Reliable Travel Methods

Responsible travel behavior may greatly lessen your influence on the environment. Observe the following advice:

- Avoid single-use plastics by carrying a reusable water bottle, shopping bag, and utensils. Select goods with little to no packaging, and place garbage in designated recycling containers.

- When leaving your hotel room, turn off the lights and the air conditioning to save electricity and water. By taking shorter showers and reusing towels, you may reduce your water use.

- Respect the local animals and the environment by staying on authorized routes and abiding by regulations for wildlife protection. Keep your distance from the wildlife, plants, and environments.

- Choose locally owned stores, eateries, and lodging to support your neighborhood and the local economy. Be courteous and meaningful in your relationships with the neighborhood.

2. Environmentally friendly lodging and dining options

Making the switch to eco-friendly hotels and restaurants is a big step towards sustainable travel. Think about the following choices:

- Hotels that prioritize sustainability practices, such as water conservation, trash reduction, and energy-efficient lighting, are considered to be eco-friendly. Seek accommodations that have eco-certifications like LEED or Green Key.

- Consider staying at farm stays or eco-lodges that support sustainable agriculture, make use of renewable energy sources, and provide an opportunity to discover the local environment and customs.

- Explore Luxembourg City's expanding selection of eateries that provide vegetarian and vegan food. These places support ethical and sustainable food options while having a less carbon impact.

- Look for restaurants that place a high priority on using organic and locally produced goods. You may help reduce the carbon emissions linked to food transportation by patronizing businesses that support sustainable agriculture.

3. Ecologically Friendly Transport

Sustainable transport choices allow you to travel around Luxembourg City with less of an environmental impact. This is how:

- **Public transportation:** Take advantage of Luxembourg City's well-connected and effective public transit system. The city and its environs may be conveniently explored via the buses and trains, which are often accessible.

- **Biking and walking**: Walking is the best method to move about Luxembourg City since it is pedestrian-friendly and small. Another eco-friendly choice is to rent a bicycle, which lets you explore the city at your leisure while reducing traffic and pollution.

- **Car-sharing and electric vehicles**: If you need to hire a car, think about going with an electric or hybrid model. Car-sharing programmes also eliminate the necessity for private auto ownership by providing on-demand access to automobiles.

- **Reduce carbon emissions**: If you're traveling to Luxembourg City, think about reducing your emissions by assisting verified carbon offset initiatives. There are several solutions available from airlines to offset the environmental effect of your trips.

You may lessen your environmental impact while also helping to preserve Luxembourg City's natural and cultural legacy by implementing these sustainable travel habits. Never forget that even tiny efforts may have a major impact on sustainable travel. Let's embrace responsible tourism and make a difference where we go.

7. USEFUL PHRASES AND VOCABULARIES

Having a few essential words and phrases in your language toolbox will substantially improve your trip to Luxembourg City. The official language of Luxembourg is Luxembourgish, although French and German are also frequently spoken. Here are some typical words and phrases to help you communicate and get about while you're here.

1. Common Luxembourgish Expressions

Germanic and Romance languages are the ancestors of Luxembourgish, a distinctive tongue. Even though English is widely spoken, making an effort to speak some Luxembourgish may help you connect with people and demonstrate that you are interested in their culture. Here are a few such sayings:

- Greetings, Moien (moy-en)
- Gratitude - Merci (mer-see)
- Indeed, Jo (yo)
- Nee (nee) - No
- Verzeihung, please (ver-zay-oong)
- Please - When will you lift? (Van Eck Guelph)
- Et tut mir leed (et toot mer last) means "I'm sorry."
- Are you an English speaker? - Do you speak English well? (sheets der English-lesh)

- What is the price? - Who will say that? (Vey Feel Khasht Daht)
- In which loo are you? - What is the toilet? Woo has, to let

2. Foundational German and French Phrases

The official language of Luxembourg is Luxembourgish, however French and German are also widely spoken in Luxembourg City. When communicating with locals, knowing some fundamental words in these languages might be helpful. A few words in French and German are as follows:

- **French:**

Bonjour (bon-zahoor) and Thank you (merci) (mer-see)

Yes, please (wee).

Non (john) - No

I'm sorry; excuse me. (ex-koo-zay-mwa)

Please (spelt with the voo) -

I apologise - Je suis désolé (huh suh day-lay)

Are you an English speaker? - Do you speak English? (par-lay voo ahn-Glay) What is the price? How much does it cost? (Koot-bee-ehn sah-Koot)

In which loo are you? - Where are the restrooms? (Oo Sohn Lay Thawl)

- **German**:

Hello, and happy day to you.

Grazie - Danke (dahn-kuh)

Yes, Ja, Ya.

No, nein (9).

Pardon me - Sincere apologies (ent-school-dee-goong)

Bitte (bit-tech), please

Es tut mir (es tut mir lot) means "I'm sorry."

Are you an English speaker? - Do you speak English? English: (share-khen zed)

What is the price? How much does it cost? (vee feel kos-tags)

In which loo are you? Where is the loo? Vo Ist De Toy Let Uh

You may demonstrate respect for the local culture and improve the quality of your relationships by learning a few words in the language and employing them. Though many individuals in Luxembourg City know English and will be pleased to help you, don't worry if you're not proficient.

7. CONCLUSION

In conclusion, Luxembourg City is a fascinating location that provides visitors with a variety of experiences. The city has much to offer every tourist, from its rich history and cultural legacy to its breathtaking architecture and natural beauty. You can fully experience Luxembourg City's charm by touring the city's finest attractions, neighborhoods, and parks.

Additionally, you may maximize your vacation by participating in a variety of activities and day excursions. There are many chances for adventure and discovery, from walking and bicycling tours to nighttime city exploration and wine-tasting excursions in the scenic Moselle Valley.

A hassle-free travel requires practical knowledge, and being aware of your lodging alternatives, the local transit options, and local traditions and etiquette may improve your experience. It's crucial to be organized and knowledgeable about the logistical details of your trip.

Any vacation to Luxembourg City should include some cultural events. There are many possibilities to immerse yourself in the city's dynamic cultural scene, from learning about Luxembourgish history and tradition to visiting festivals and events, seeing museums and galleries, taking in music and theater performances, and savoring regional cuisine.

Last but not least, incorporating sustainable habits into your trip may benefit the area's residents and ecology. You may help to preserve the city's natural beauty and cultural legacy by following responsible travel habits, selecting eco-friendly lodging and eating alternatives, and using sustainable transportation.

With the right terminology and phrases in Luxembourgish, French, and German, you may improve your interactions with locals and demonstrate your respect for their language and way of life.

Luxembourg City offers visitors a unique and remarkable experience by combining history, culture, environment, and sustainability. You'll make lifelong memories by discovering everything that this charming city has to offer. Plan your vacation now, acquaint yourself with Luxembourg City's charms, and set off on a remarkable journey.

8. APPENDIX

Every travel guide should include an appendix, which gives readers access to additional resources and information to improve their trip. You may discover maps of Luxembourg City, suggestions for reading material, a traveler's checklist, a dictionary of important phrases, and an index in this supplement.

1. Luxembourg City maps

For traveling and touring Luxembourg City, maps are a need. Here are a few suggested maps to get you around:

- **City Map**: A thorough map of Luxembourg City that shows the main thoroughfares, neighborhoods, and landmarks. You may use this map to plan your schedule and get acquainted with the layout of the city.

- **Public Transportation Map:** This map shows the locations of all the city's buses and railways. You may use this map to better comprehend the transportation system and choose the most practical routes to your preferred locations.

- **Tourist Attractions Map**: A map of Luxembourg City's key tourist destinations, including the Grand Ducal Palace Notre tre

DameCathedral, and Place d'Armes, is available here. You may find these sites on this map and use them to organize your touring schedule.

These maps are often available from hotels, tourist information offices, and official tourism websites for download.

2. Suggestions for Books and Resources

Consider examining the following publications and sources to learn more about the heritage, culture, and tourist attractions of Luxembourg City:

- **Patrick Levy's "Luxembourg City:** A Cultural and Literary History" By offering historical background and examining the literary contributions that have defined Luxembourg City, this book sheds light on the cultural history of the city.

- **Tim Skelton's "Luxembourg**: The Bradt Travel Guide": An extensive travel guide that covers the whole of Luxembourg, including information on the sights, lodging, food, and transportation in Luxembourg City.

- **Official Tourism Websites:** Visit the official tourist websites for Luxembourg City and the whole country of Luxembourg. These websites provide current information on attractions, events, travel options, and other aspects of travel.

- **Online Travel Forums and Blogs:** Participate in online travel forums and read travel blogs that are specific to Luxembourg City. These online resources help you find undiscovered jewels and off-the-beaten-path sites by sharing personal stories, ideas, and advice from other travelers.

3. Traveler's Checklist

A traveler's checklist may help you make sure everything is ready before you go to Luxembourg City. The following are some necessities to add:

- **Valid Passport**: Verify that your passport will be valid throughout your whole visit to Luxembourg City.

- **Visa Requirements:** Check your nationality's requirements to see whether you need a visa to visit Luxembourg City.

- **Travel Insurance:** Consider purchasing travel insurance to protect yourself from unforeseeable events like medical crises or trip cancellations.

- **Currency**: Become familiar with the Euro, the country's official currency, and think about packing some cash for little purchases. Additionally, to prevent any problems with card transactions, let your bank or credit card provider know about your vacation intentions.

- **Weather and Clothing:** Check the weather forecast for Luxembourg City before your trip, and bring the proper clothes and accessories.

- **Medication & prescriptions**: Make sure you have enough of any drugs you use to last the length of your vacation. It's also a good idea to have a copy of your medications with you.

- **Electronics & Adapters:** Be sure you pack the proper adapters for your electronic gadgets and research the types of electrical outlets in Luxembourg City.

- **Emergency Contacts**: Write down the numbers for your embassy or consulate, your local government, and your travel insurance company.

4. Key Terms Glossary

Here are some essential terminology to help you throughout your stay in Luxembourg City that will help you understand and communicate:

- **Hello in Luxembourgish:**

Moien (moy-en)
I'm grateful. Thank you (per-se)
Hello: (ah-dee)
I'm sorry. The word "versing"

- **French:**

Hello: Greetings (bon-shoot)
I'm grateful. Thank you (per-se)
Goodbye: At last Oh, ruh-vah-r
I'm sorry. Please excuse me (ex-koo-zay-mwa).

- **German:**

Hello: Good morning (goo-ten task)
I'm grateful. Danke (dahn-kuh)

Goodbye: Onward and upward (of vee-dhuhrzay-en)

I'm sorry. Entschuldigung (ent-school-dee-goong)

5. Index

The contents of the trip guide are quickly accessible via an index. It makes it simple for readers to find certain subjects or information they're looking for. Important landmarks, localities, useful information, cultural experiences, and any other pertinent subjects addressed in the guide may be included in the index.

Readers may search for specific information or go back to chapters they found especially helpful by using the index. It is a helpful tool for swiftly navigating the trip guide.

The appendix concludes by offering extra information, aids, and references to improve your time in Luxembourg City. A thorough and user-friendly travel guide includes various elements, such as utilizing maps for navigation, looking at suggested reading material, using a traveler's checklist, consulting a glossary of essential terminology, and using the index for rapid reference. Make the most of your time traveling around Luxembourg City and taking in this fascinating place.

Luxembourg city

Printed in Great Britain
by Amazon